3/93

MARY KAY ASH

Mary Kay—
A Beautiful
Business

MARY KAY ASH

Mary Kay—
A Beautiful
Business

Rebecca Stefoff

GEC GARRETT EDUCATIONAL CORPORATION

Cover: *Mary Kay Ash*. (Mary Kay Cosmetics, Inc.)

Edited and produced by Synthegraphics Corporation

Library of Congress Cataloging in Publication Data

Stefoff, Rebecca.
Mary Kay Ash : Mary Kay, a beautiful business / Rebecca Stefoff.
    p. cm. — (Wizards of business)
  Includes index.
  Summary: A biography of the woman who began her own cosmetic business to put her business philosopy into work.
  ISBN 1-56074-012-4
  1. Ash, Mary Kay—Juvenile literature. 2. Mary Kay Cosmetics—History—Juvenile literature. 3. Cosmetics industry—United States—History—Juvenile literature. 4. Industrialists—United States—Biography—Juvenile literature. 5. Women in business—United States—Juvenile literature. [1. Ash, Mary Kay. 2. Businesswomen. 3. Mary Kay Cosmetics—History.] I. Title. II. Series.
HD9970.5.C672A837   1992
381'.456685'092—dc20   91-32055
[B]   CIP
                                                           AC

921
Ash

Contents

Chronology for **Mary Kay Ash**

1919?	Born Mary Kathlyn Wagner in Hot Wells, Texas
1936?	Married Ben Rogers
1942?- **1963**	Worked in direct sales selling products to people at home
1953	Began practicing the skin-care program that eventually became the basis for her own business
1963	After death of second husband, started a company called Beauty by Mary Kay (name later changed to Mary Kay Cosmetics, Inc.)
1966	Married Mel Ash
1968	Mary Kay Cosmetics became a publicly owned corporation
1976	Honored by *Business Week* magazine as one of America's Top 100 Corporate Women; appointed to the Direct Marketing Association's Hall of Fame
1980	After Mel Ash died of lung cancer, Mary Kay began a program of funding cancer research and treatment
1982	Wrote autobiography
1984	Wrote *Mary Kay on People Management,* which became a best-seller
1985	Company returned to private ownership
1987	Named chairman emeritus of company

Chapter 1

"You Can Do It, Mary Kay!"

One day in 1963, a woman named Mary Kay quit her job. She held a high-ranking position working for a company called World Gift in Dallas, Texas, that sold home accessories all across the United States. She had worked for the company for nine years, first as a salesperson and later as a trainer of other salespeople.

Before that, Mary Kay had worked for thirteen years for a company called Stanley Home Products, which sold items such as cleaning supplies and other household goods to house-wives. All in all, Mary Kay had spent about twenty-two years in the sales business when she quit her job at World Gift.

Many people would have thought that almost twenty-five years of selling products was enough of a career. They would have settled down to a quiet retirement – but not Mary

Kay. Although she was middle-aged, she had more energy than most people half her age, and she was full of good ideas that she wanted to put to use.

A WOMAN IN A MAN'S WORLD

In fact, one of the reasons Mary Kay had left her job at World Gift was because she felt that the top bosses in the company were not willing to listen to her ideas about how to manage people. They didn't take her seriously when she made suggestions that she thought would save the company money and inspire its salespeople. Later, remembering her frustration at that time, she said, "I became enraged every time I presented a good **marketing** plan and was dismissed with, 'Mary Kay, you're thinking just like a woman.' " (Terms in **boldface type** are defined in the Glossary at the back of this book.)

Mary Kay also hated the fact that nearly all of the most powerful people in the business world were men who did not really believe in treating women equally. Often, during her career, she had worked harder and earned more money for her company than a male employee, but was paid less because she was a woman.

In recent years, women have begun to move closer to equal rights with men in the working world. But during Mary Kay's sales career, business was very much "a man's world." Mary Kay said years later, "Much of the time I was actually handicapped or held back by outdated ideas of what a woman should and should not do when working with men."

It made Mary Kay particularly furious when a man she herself had trained was given a promotion that turned him into her boss – with a salary twice as big as hers. This happened more than once, and it was one of the things that made her fed up with working in other people's companies.

DREAMING UP A DREAM COMPANY

In spite of Mary Kay's abundant energy, the last thing she planned to do when she left her job at World Gift in 1963 was to start a business of her own. Instead, she decided to write a book based on her experiences as a salesperson and a trainer. She wanted to express her ideas about how a successful business might be organized and operated.

Mary Kay also wanted to share her thoughts on how women could overcome some of the obstacles she had run into during her career. Finally, she hoped that writing about work would help her get rid of some of the anger and bitterness she felt about the barriers and limitations she had encountered as a career woman.

Two Lists

Mary Kay sat down at her kitchen table and started working on two long lists. One of them was a list of positive things. It included all of the good, encouraging, or rewarding experiences she had enjoyed while working, as well as all of the good features of the companies that she knew well. The other list contained negative things, such as setbacks she had suffered and features of companies that she thought could be improved.

One thing that has made Mary Kay so successful, though, is that she doesn't simply complain about what's wrong – she does her best to figure out how to fix it. So whenever she listed something negative about a company or a business experience, she also wrote down how she would improve that particular thing, or how it could be done differently.

The Golden Rule – A Business Philosophy

According to Mary Kay, the basis for her **business philosophy** was the simple, old-fashioned principle that is sometimes called the golden rule. This rule says: Do unto others as you would have them do unto you. "I felt a business should be conducted in accordance with the golden rule," she says. "If an employer would treat employees and customers as he or she would wish to be treated – all would **profit**."

Something unexpected happened as Mary Kay worked on these ideas for her book. "As my list grew," she says, "I began to dream of a company in which women had the opportunity to fully utilize their skills and talents. They could, in fact, enjoy the rewards for any goal they were smart enough to reach."

Before long, Mary Kay found herself wishing that someone would start a company just like the one she was describing. "I'd love to work for an organization like this," she would say to herself as she sat at her kitchen table reading over her lists and plans.

Mary Kay Ash at her office in Dallas. She established her successful cosmetics company based on her own personal experiences in direct sales. She also wanted to provide women with an opportunity to utilize their skills and talents. (Shelly Katz/Black Star.)

It wasn't long before Mary Kay took the next step — realizing that she could start her own "dream company." This idea filled her with excitement and enthusiasm. What a thrill it would be to put her own thoughts about business into practice, to try and make them work — and perhaps to help other women succeed in business as well.

Mary Kay was not simply a dreamer, however. She was also a practical, hardheaded businesswoman with almost twenty-five years of experience in selling different products. So she knew that her venture with her "dream company" would have to be more than just a hopeful experiment. Before she would **invest** her time and money in a company of her own, she would want to be very sure that it had a good chance of making money. And in order to do that, she realized, she needed more than a list of ideas about running a business. She also needed something to sell.

FINDING THE RIGHT PRODUCT

Mary Kay needed a **product** that would be **competitive.** For people to want to buy it, it had to be either something that was completely new, or something that was better than other similar products. Brand-new ideas and products are pretty rare.

Fortunately, however, Mary Kay already knew of a product that she thought people would buy. She had been using it herself for more than ten years. The product that Mary Kay had in mind was a set of skin creams and lotions that she had discovered when she was selling Stanley Home Products in the early 1950s.

One evening back then, Mary Kay was giving a home show, or demonstration party, for about twenty women who might be interested in buying some of the Stanley products. The show was in the home of a woman who had invited her friends to see Mary Kay's sales presentation. The guests ranged in age from nineteen to seventy years old.

As she looked around the room, Mary Kay gradually noticed that, despite their differences in age, all the women had one thing in common – beautiful, young-looking skin. After she finished her presentation, she noticed that the hostess was passing out small bottles and jars with handwritten labels to the guests. She decided that those mysterious little bottles must be the source of the perfect complexions she had been noticing, so she asked the hostess to explain.

A Tanner's Discovery

Mary Kay learned that the hostess' father had been a tanner, whose job was turning animal hides into leather. After years of working with the chemicals used in tanning, this man had noticed that his hands were smoother, softer, and younger looking than his face, so he started using the tanning solutions on his face. When he died at the age of seventy-three, his daughter said, her father's skin looked like the skin of a much younger man.

The daughter had studied **cosmetology** and had managed to develop formulas that were similar to her father's tanning solutions but were gentler and easier to use. These were the contents of the five little jars and bottles that Mary Kay had seen the hostess handing out to the women.

Mary Kay was a little doubtful about trying these "home-made" skin-care products. Nevertheless, she took a set of them home with her that night in a shoebox. A few days later, she gave herself a facial with the new products. When her ten-year-old son Richard came home from school that day, he kissed her on the cheek and then surprised her by saying, "Gee, Mom, you feel smooth!" As Mary Kay says, "I knew right then that I was on to something."

For more than ten years since that time, Mary Kay faithfully used the items made by the tanner's daughter. But the products were not completely delightful to use. "They were dark orange and smelled like a skunk," Mary Kay recalls, "but they made my skin so soft. I'd be giving a Stanley demonstration, and a client would say, 'We know about that bowl cleaner, tell us what you've done to your face.' "

Mary Kay even introduced her mother to the skin-care products. She reports that although her mother was eighty-seven years old when she died, her skin was so soft and youthful that most people thought she was only about sixty years old.

STARTING A NEW CAREER

From her own experience, then, Mary Kay knew that these skin-care products worked. She also knew that it would be easy to interest people in buying them. In addition, she wanted to work with women, and she realized that women could comfortably sell cosmetic products to other women.

So, when Mary Kay started thinking about forming her own "dream company" in 1963, it was natural for her to think of the items made by the tanner's daughter as a product line that could form the basis for the company. She felt that if she invested her ideas, her time, and a certain amount of money for producing and packaging the items, she could turn the skin-care products into a much bigger business than their original owner had ever done.

This is how it came about that only four weeks after leaving her job at World Gift, Mary Kay was planning to start a whole new career. But this time she would not be just a salesperson or an employee. Rather, she would be the head of her own company.

The first step was to obtain the right to use the formulas that the tanner and his daughter had developed. Mary Kay bought the recipes from the tanner's daughter, then she started planning to get her new company, which she called Beauty by Mary Kay, off the ground.

Mary Kay received a lot of help from her husband, who was an **executive** at a company that sold vitamins. He handled the parts of the planning that involved financial and legal details, while Mary Kay concentrated on developing her ideas for **recruiting,** training, and managing people. Then, just one month before the company was scheduled to go into business, tragedy struck.

A TURNING POINT

Mary Kay and her husband were having breakfast together one day when his face suddenly turned purple and he fell forward onto the table. She jumped up at once to call an ambulance, but he was beyond help. He had suffered a fatal heart attack.

In the midst of grieving for her husband, Mary Kay had to make a very serious decision. Should she continue with their plans for Beauty by Mary Kay alone? They had already paid to have batches of the products made, along with new bottles and labels. All of that would be wasted if she did not open the business as planned. But she had always counted on her husband's help in managing the company.

Mary Kay asked her lawyer and her accountant for advice. Both of them told her to scrap her plans for the company then and there. They said that her ideas would never work, that Beauty by Mary Kay would go out of business. "You'll end up penniless," her lawyer warned.

But Mary Kay listened to another voice, one that seemed to be coming from deep inside her. It gave her confidence and made her believe that she could do anything she put her mind to. This voice was that of her mother, and it spoke to her from childhood memories, saying, "You *can* do it, Mary Kay!"

Chapter 2

Childhood Challenges

Mary Kay was born Mary Kathlyn Wagner in a small Texas town called Hot Wells. Because she does not like her age to be known, she never tells the year of her birth, but it was probably around 1919.

The childhoods of successful people are often colorful and interesting to read about. Mary Kay's childhood is especially important because while she was growing up she learned several lessons that have shaped her life and her business career ever since. In fact, she says that she began learning the secrets of success at a very early age.

KEEPING HOUSE

When Mary Kay was two years old, her father became ill with a lung disease called tuberculosis. The medical treatment for this disease required him to stay for some time at a special hospital called a sanatorium. He returned home when Mary Kay was seven years old, but the doctors had been unable to cure him. He was an invalid for the rest of his life and needed a lot of care.

Mary Kay's mother had to work to support the family. She had been trained as a nurse, but she found a job as the manager of a restaurant in Houston, Texas. She had to work long hours, usually sixteen hours a day, from five in the morning until nine at night. This meant that she had to leave home before Mary Kay woke up and often did not return until after Mary Kay was asleep.

Shouldering Responsibilities

Mary Kay had an older brother and sister. But because both of them were grown up and had moved away, the responsibility of caring for her father fell upon her young shoulders. She also had to take care of herself much of the time. Fortunately, she had a loving, patient mother who did her best to make things easier.

After coming home from school, Mary Kay would first clean the house, then she would do her homework. This didn't leave her with much time to play with her friends or even by herself. But, as Mary Kay recalls, she not only accepted her responsibilities around the house, she even enjoyed them. As she said later, "Even though some of my duties were supposed to be too difficult for a child, nobody ever told me that. As a result, I just *did* them."

Cooking and Shopping

Cooking was one of Mary Kay's biggest challenges. Her mother could not be home to show Mary Kay how to prepare meals, but she gave her cooking lessons over the telephone. Mary Kay remembers that if her father wanted potato soup, for example, she would telephone her mother at the restaurant, and her mother would say, "Okay, honey. First get out the big pot, the one you used last night. Then take two potatoes . . ." And Mary Kay's mother always ended the conversation with these words: "Honey, I know you can do it."

The same thing happened when Mary Kay needed clothes for school. Her mother would give her the money to buy a new blouse or dress and then carefully explain to her how to get downtown on the streetcar. The little girl would follow her mother's directions and go to the stores to make her purchases. Sometimes the salesclerks could not believe that such a small child was allowed to shop by herself. Mary Kay would give them the telephone number of her mother's restaurant and say, "Call her. She'll tell you it's okay."

Whenever Mary Kay became nervous about getting lost, she would remember her mother saying, "I know you can do it," and she'd do fine. Later, when Mary Kay grew up and had children of her own, she realized how much her mother must have worried about giving so much responsibility to her little girl. But she never let Mary Kay see her concern. Instead, she showed only confidence, and Mary Kay says that her mother's confidence in her has stayed with her all through her life. Whenever someone said to her, "You can't," Mary Kay would be reminded of her mother's voice saying, "You *can!*"

LEARNING TO COMPETE

Self-confidence was only one of the lessons that Mary Kay learned from her mother as she was growing up. She also learned how to compete, with others and with herself. Because her mother was proud of her, she worked hard to get straight A's in her classes at school or to sell the most boxes of Girl Scout cookies.

Mary Kay succeeded at almost everything she tried. She discovered that the true joy of competition does not lie in doing better than everyone else. Instead, it lies in simply doing your best, or competing with your own past achievements.

Success from Failure

But because no one can be a winner all the time, Mary Kay's mother wisely taught her daughter how to lose as well as how to win. She encouraged Mary Kay to view each setback or failure as an opportunity to learn something so that she could do better the next time. This philosophy is summed up in one of Mary Kay's favorite sayings, which is, "We fail forward to success." She believes that successes are built on past failures, and that the people who succeed in reaching their goals are those who keep trying.

In junior high school, Mary Kay discovered one area in which she loved to compete, and that was typing. She took a typing class and, with typical determination and ambition, she decided to excel at typing. What she wanted most in the world was a typewriter of her own, but she knew that her family could not afford it.

To Mary Kay's astonishment, however, one day her mother presented her with a typewriter. "To this day," says Mary Kay, "I can't imagine how she was able to save enough money for the down payment, or how long it must have taken her to pay for that wonderful machine." Mary Kay showed her gratitude by bringing home the trophy for being the best typist in her class.

Important Friendships

Two friends from Mary Kay's schooldays helped shape her life. One of them was a girl named Tillie Bass. Tillie and her mother often helped Mary Kay with advice on cooking and the other chores she had to do around the house. Because Tillie was a little older than Mary Kay, the younger girl was proud of the friendship and worked hard to keep up with Tillie in school and in the homemaking skills that the two girls learned together.

Later, when Mary Kay was a young working mother, Tillie helped again by taking care of Mary Kay's children. In the 1980s, after she had become a millionaire in the cosmetics business, Mary Kay was able to repay the kindness Tillie had shown over the years of their friendship. She invited Tillie and her husband to share her large new home in Dallas, Texas.

Another good friend from Mary Kay's early years was Dorothy Zapp. The two girls engaged in friendly competition until high school, when Dorothy moved away and went to a

Mary Kay at her high school graduation. She had hoped to go to college, but her mother could not afford it. The country was in the midst of the Great Depression, and times were hard. (Mary Kay Cosmetics, Inc.)

different school. Mary Kay finished high school in three years by attending summer school. She wanted to go to college, but her mother simply could not afford it.

AN EARLY MARRIAGE

As Mary Kay watched Dorothy and many of her other friends go away to college, she felt what she later described as "my first experience of envy." Unfortunately for Mary Kay, her envy of the other young people who were able to go to college made her do something rather foolish. She wanted to compete with them and make a bit of a splash, so, at age seventeen, she got married.

Mary Kay's husband, a young man named Ben Rogers, sang on the radio in a group called the Hawaiian Strummers. He also worked in a gas station. "I thought he was a real catch," she recalls, "sort of the Elvis Presley of the time. Maybe I couldn't go to college, but there was no doubt that *this* was a real feather in my cap!"

Mary Kay now admits that the competitive spirit that drove her to make such an early marriage created "a real problem" for her, for the marriage was not a happy one. At first, she and Ben lived in a bedroom at her mother's house in Houston. They eventually moved into a home of their own and started raising a family. They had three children, Marylyn, Ben, and Richard.

After Ben got a job in Dallas, the young Rogers family

moved there. But by this time, Ben and Mary Kay were having serious marriage problems. Then Ben was called away to serve in the Army in World War II.

Mary Kay now found herself in the same position that her mother had been in not so long before. She was responsible for finding work and paying her family's bills. Only this family consisted of not one but three small children!

Chapter 3

Discovering Direct Sales

To support her family while her husband was in the Army, Mary Kay turned to those typing skills that she had been so proud of back in junior high school. She found a job as a secretary. But before long, she turned to **direct sales** as a way to have flexible working hours so that she could be home when her children needed her. In fact, she had already had several experiences in selling. Each of these experiences taught her lessons that she later put to use in her own company.

THE POWER OF ENTHUSIASM

One day, while still living in Houston with her husband and young children, Mary Kay received a visit from a door-to-door saleswoman named Ida Blake. Ida was selling a series of children's books called the *Child Psychology Bookshelf*. "I thought those were the best books I had ever seen," Mary Kay remembers. "Unfortunately, I couldn't afford them."

Ida Blake let Mary Kay keep the books over the weekend. As she read them all from cover to cover, Mary Kay grew still more excited about them. When Ida arrived to pick up the books, Mary Kay told her that she intended to save up her money until she could afford to buy them. Ida saw that Mary Kay was brimming with enthusiasm and offered, "If you sell 10 sets for me, I'll give you a set."

Mary Kay promptly got on the phone and called the parents of all the children in the Sunday School class she taught at her Baptist church. In a day and a half, she had sold all ten sets! And she didn't even have a sample set of books to show people – all she had was her enthusiasm. But it worked. Ida was so impressed that she offered Mary Kay a job.

Two Important Lessons

In nine months, Mary Kay sold $25,000 worth of books. She learned two things from this job. The first lesson was how powerful her enthusiasm could be when she used it to communicate her excitement and her belief in a product's value.

Mary Kay learned the second lesson when she met some of her customers afterward and discovered that they were not using the books they had bought from her. Some of them even blamed her for "talking them into" buying books that sat on the shelves and were never read.

Mary Kay realized that this was not her fault. She still believed that the books were a good, valuable product. But she decided that even the best product was not going to make people happy unless the person who sold it to them also *taught* them how to make the best use of it.

This principle later became the main selling technique of the Mary Kay Cosmetics sales force. Mary Kay skin-care products and cosmetics cannot be purchased in stores. Instead, salespeople called "beauty consultants" demonstrate the products in the homes of persons who are interested in them. The demonstration includes a complete lesson in how to use the products for best results.

THE HARD SELL

Soon after Mary Kay's experience with the *Child Psychology Bookshelf,* her husband lost his job at the gas station. The two of them then teamed up on another direct sales job. They went into people's homes and sold sets of high-quality pots and pans at dinner parties to which several married couples had been invited.

To do this, Mary Kay performed cooking demonstrations in the customers' kitchens. She always prepared the same thing: ham, green beans, sweet potatoes, and a cake. She became very good at cooking those particular foods!

While her husband was in the living room, trying to talk the men into buying the cookware sets, Mary Kay was in the kitchen, showing the wives how easy it was to cook perfect dinners with them. But Mary Kay and her husband couldn't afford to buy the food for themselves. So, if there was anything left over after the demonstration, it became their dinner. However, if the people at the party ate it all, Mary Kay and Ben just didn't eat that night.

More Important Lessons

This job taught Mary Kay a couple of things, too. First of all, the country was in the grip of the **Great Depression** of the 1930s. During this time, most people simply did not have enough money to buy an expensive item like a new set of cookware. Because Mary Kay and her husband could not make enough sales, they had to quit. As a result, she learned that it was not enough for a product to be good. It also had to be affordable, so that enough people would buy it. And it had to be something that people would probably continue to buy even during hard times.

Skin creams and makeup fall into this category. In fact, cosmetics are sometimes called a "depression-proof" industry because a woman who cannot afford a new dress or a piece of jewelry will often cheer herself up by buying makeup, which is less expensive. Economic history has shown that even when money is scarce, people still buy cosmetics, just as they still go to movies.

The cookware job also taught Mary Kay a second lesson. It introduced her to the sales method called the **hard sell,**

Mary Kay Cosmetics uses the system of sales "parties" that Mary Kay perfected while she was working for Stanley Home Products. Here, a Mary Kay saleswoman, or beauty consultant, demonstrates products at a sales party in Virginia. (Christopher Casler.)

and she decided that she didn't like it. When she later formed her own company, she based it on the **soft sell.** She didn't want customers to see dollar signs in her salespeople's eyes. Instead, she wanted them to feel relaxed and comfortable.

LESSONS IN MOTIVATION

While her husband was in the Army, Mary Kay went to work as a saleswoman for a company called Stanley Home Products. She would contact a friend, or a friend of a friend, and offer to give a demonstration of the company's products in the woman's home to a group of the woman's acquaintances. These shows were called "parties." At each party, Mary Kay would try to sell the cleansers and other items in her product line.

Mary Kay also used all her powers of enthusiasm and communication to recruit people who attended the parties into becoming salespeople themselves. This was because of what she calls "that old competitive spirit." Stanley announced that it planned to award a prize and the title "Miss Dallas" to the salesperson who brought in the most new recruits. Mary Kay met the challenge and won the contest. From this and other contests, she learned that people will often work just as hard for public recognition and praise as they will for money.

The Queen of Sales

Mary Kay quickly became very good at selling Stanley Home Products, but when she started out she had a lot to learn. When she heard that the company was holding a convention in Dallas, she borrowed twelve dollars so that she could attend. (She didn't know if the price of the convention included food, so she took some cheese and crackers with her, and that's what she lived on for three days. To this day, she likes to send cheese and crackers to the rooms of people attending Mary Kay meetings.)

At the convention, Mary Kay saw the year's top saleswoman crowned "Queen of Sales" and awarded a beautiful,

Mary Kay is shown here preparing buttons for the guests at a special meeting to recognize the achievements of top salespeople and recruiters. From the start, Mary Kay strongly believed in showing public appreciation for outstanding work. (Mary Kay Cosmetics, Inc.)

expensive, alligator-skin handbag. At that moment, Mary Kay vowed to herself that *she* would be the next year's Queen of Sales, even though at the time she was only making about seven dollars a week in sales.

Hoping to learn how to be a winner, Mary Kay persuaded the "Queen" to give a demonstration for her. She then took careful notes of everything this successful saleswoman said and did. Throughout the following year, Mary Kay modeled her sales technique on that of the Queen. She clipped a photograph of an alligator handbag out of a magazine and carried it around in her purse to **motivate** her.

Direct Sales

Direct sales is nothing more than a type of selling that takes place directly between a salesperson and a customer, not in a store. In addition to Mary Kay Cosmetics, some well-known products that are sold through direct sales are Avon cosmetics, Tupperware plastic kitchenware, Amway soaps and household products, and many kinds of books, especially Bibles and encyclopedias.

In direct sales, the salesperson usually contacts the customer. This used to be done through door-to-door selling, which is sometimes called "cold canvassing." A door-to-door salesperson simply goes from house to house, ringing doorbells and usually talking to housewives. This type of selling is becoming less common because so many women work outside the home today, and also because people are more cautious about letting strangers into their homes.

Two types of direct sales that are more common today are called "networking" and "party planning." In networking, a salesperson makes individual presentations but usually makes them by appointment, starting with friends or acquaintances and then getting referrals to *their* friends. In the party-plan system, the salesperson helps one potential customer arrange a group demonstration, with the idea that some of the guests at the "party" will want to host demonstrations at their own homes.

In addition to these types of direct sales, many people who have jobs in offices and other places of business also work in direct sales part-time, and sometimes they are able to sell their products to their co-workers during their lunch hours or on coffee breaks. In fact, more than half of the people who represent direct-sales companies do so part-time, either in addition to their full-time jobs or, in the case of many women who have children, as a way of earning some extra money without the demands of a full-time job.

Sure enough, when the next convention rolled around, Mary Kay was crowned Queen of Sales! To her dismay, however, the prize had been changed. She did not win the alligator bag after all. She doesn't remember what the prize was, but she remembers that it wasn't the bag.

Prizes that Women Value

Later, in another contest, Mary Kay won something called a flounder light. It appeared completely useless. For years, she didn't even know what it was. Finally, she learned that it was a light to use in night fishing – something she had no interest in doing!

This experience taught Mary Kay that rewards should be something that the winner will truly prize. For that reason, Mary Kay Cosmetics is structured around many levels of achievement, with public recognition for those who reach various sales amounts. And the prizes that Mary Kay awards are things that she believes most women enjoy, such as fur coats, diamond jewelry, and cars.

The cars are probably the most famous symbol of Mary Kay, because all of them are painted in the company's trademark shade of pink! The General Motors Company even has a special shade of auto paint that it calls Mary Kay Pink.

CHANGES IN DIRECTION

Mary Kay now says that the most exhausting period of her life came when she was twenty-seven years old and had been married for ten years. Her husband was still in the Army, and she was working as a Stanley representative, arranging her parties around her children's school schedule. She decided to take on another role – that of college student.

For a long time, Mary Kay had dreamed of becoming a doctor, so she enrolled in a college program that would prepare her for medical school. Her schedule was hectic. She had classes in the morning and a Stanley party every afternoon. Then, when she arrived home, she would cook, clean, and serve dinner to the children. By the end of the day, she was too tired to study. She started getting up at three in the morning to hit the books, and before long she was on the verge of collapse.

Life Strikes a Blow

Around this time Mary Kay suffered a dreadful blow. Her husband returned from the Army and told her that he wanted a divorce. He had fallen in love with another woman. That was the lowest point of Mary Kay's life. "I felt like a complete and total failure," she now says.

Getting a divorce meant that staying in school would be harder than ever for Mary Kay, who would need to earn more money to support the children. She also discovered from a series of tests she took at school that her talents for persuasion and communication were far greater than her scientific abilities.

The dean of Mary Kay's school pointed out that it would be many years before she would complete her medical studies. He advised her to consider a career in sales, where she could put her skills to use right away. Mary Kay knew that this was good advice, because she already had a flourishing part-time sales career! So she left school and turned her attention to full-time selling for Stanley Home Products and taking care of her family.

Thinking Positive

Mary Kay's sadness over her divorce, along with the strain of being responsible for her children, had an effect on her health. She began to experience pain and other symptoms. Doctors told her that she had arthritis and that she would probably be completely disabled within just a few months!

This prospect seemed unthinkable to Mary Kay. She decided to try as hard as possible to give three Stanley parties every day, and to be cheerful and smiling at each one of them, no matter how bad she felt. Gradually, as her parties became more and more successful, the symptoms of illness went away.

Mary Kay's doctors warned her that the arthritis would return, but it never did. She is convinced that her illness was caused by stress and a negative mental attitude, and that she "cured" it by thinking positive.

TIME-MANAGEMENT SKILLS

During the years that followed, Mary Kay's busy schedule left her time for just three things: church, family, and work. She developed a number of ways to make the best use of her time, and these became lifelong habits.

For one thing, Mary Kay learned to **delegate.** Remembering all of the things she had done to help her mother when she was a child, she got her own children involved in some of the tasks she had to do. For example, on Saturday afternoons, she and the children would sit down and go over the orders she had taken at Stanley parties during the week. The children would help her pack the items for each order. Then they would add up the money she had brought home and figure out the profit.

Mary Kay feels that this activity taught her children the basics of good business sense. Her son Richard started helping her when he was only six years old. Today, he is the chairman of Mary Kay Cosmetics.

Mary Kay also gave each child chores to do around the house. She rewarded good performance with an allowance. This was her way of teaching them something she believes is a vital lesson: You get out of life what you put into it. If you don't do good work, you cannot expect a reward.

Hiring a Housekeeper

But Mary Kay knew that the children couldn't do everything, so she hired a housekeeper. This was a daring step, because Mary Kay didn't even have the money to pay a housekeeper when she ran an ad in the newspaper. However, she believed that if she had a housekeeper, she could give more Stanley parties and earn enough money to pay for the housekeeper.

When a woman appeared to apply for the job, Mary Kay hired her – and then went out to work, hoping to earn the money that day to pay her! The plan succeeded. Each week, Mary Kay devoted one day to earning her housekeeper's pay, and the same woman continued to work for her for nine years.

Another time trick that Mary Kay taught herself was something that she calls the Five O'Clock Club. She discovered that if she trained herself to get up at five each morning, before the children were awake and long before the telephone started ringing, she could get a lot of paperwork done. She still gets up at five every day and uses that quiet time to write letters, read reports, and organize herself for the day ahead.

The $35,000 List

According to Mary Kay, one of the most important secrets to being successful – whether at work, at school, or at managing a home and family – is being organized. When she was just beginning her sales career, she read something that has helped her organize her business ever since.

What Mary Kay read was a story about Ivy Lee, who was a well-known **efficiency expert,** and Charles Schwab, who was the president of Bethlehem Steel. Lee told Schwab that if he let her spend fifteen minutes coaching his top executives, she could increase his company's efficiency and also its earnings. Schwab asked what her services would cost. Lee replied that she would give him three months to decide how valuable her advice was, and then he could send her a check for whatever amount he thought was fair.

Schwab agreed, and Ivy Lee proceeded to give the company's executives a single piece of advice. She told them to make a list every evening of the six most important things they had to accomplish the next day, in order of importance. Then, each executive was to come to work each day and tackle those six jobs, one by one, finishing each before moving on to the next.

Three months later, Charles Schwab mailed Ivy Lee a check for $35,000. That's how valuable he thought her advice had been. This story made a profound impact on Mary Kay. She realized that making such a list would help her decide what was really most important in her life. It would keep her from wasting her time on minor concerns that did not move her toward her goals. So she has used the "$35,000 list" throughout her career. It is a piece of advice she often passes on to the employees and beauty consultants who work for Mary Kay Cosmetics.

Chapter 4

The Dream Company

Mary Kay proved to be an outstanding representative for Stanley Home Products. Not only did she sell a lot of products, but she was also good at recruiting other salespeople. Recruiting was a big part of her job, because she earned a **commission** on all the money that was brought into the company by people she had recruited in her territory.

Over the years Mary Kay has perfected her sales technique. One secret to her success, though, is that she didn't simply reach a high level of performance and then stay there – she always kept trying to do better. She believes that one characteristic of successful people who are happy with their lives is that they keep challenging themselves, pushing themselves to learn and grow. So when Mary Kay tried something that didn't work, she made a plan to do better next time. And even when she tried something that *did* work, she also made a plan to do better next time!

NEGATIVE EXPERIENCES

Although she had many triumphs with Stanley Home Products, Mary Kay also encountered many frustrations. One thing she didn't like was the system of assigned territories. Each salesperson was assigned a territory by the company. This meant that Mary Kay could work only inside her own territory. So, when she remarried and her second husband was transferred to St. Louis, Missouri, she lost the territory she had built up in Dallas. "I lost all the commissions on the people I had recruited, trained, and motivated for eight years," she says. "I thought this was [very] unfair. I had built the territory, but someone else inherited all those terrific salespeople, *and* the commissions on their sales."

A New Sales System

Nearly all sales organizations use the system of assigned territories. But years later, when she began thinking about her own "dream company," Mary Kay decided that assigned territories were not necessary. She felt a company would work just fine if every salesperson could sell the product anywhere – at home, on vacation, or wherever he or she happened to be. And any salesperson could recruit a new salesperson anywhere.

To illustrate her point, Mary Kay came up with this example: A woman who sold the product in Cleveland could be visiting her sister in Omaha and could recruit a new salesperson there. When the first woman returned to Cleveland, the new recruit would be trained by the sales director in the Omaha region. However, commissions on the recruit's sales would go to the woman in Cleveland. In the meantime, the sales director in Omaha might well be receiving commissions from her own recruits in other cities across the country.

Business advisors claimed that this system would never work, but Mary Kay thought that it would. And it *has* worked in Mary Kay's company. Everyone is willing to help other people's recruits, because *everyone* continues to earn commissions on the sales made by his or her *own* recruits, no matter where they are.

Facing Prejudice

Even more infuriating than the issue of assigned territories was the prejudice that many men in business showed toward Mary Kay as she became increasingly successful. Mary Kay felt that most men did not welcome women into the work force. They seemed to believe that women were not serious about having careers but only wanted to work until they got married or had children. Mary Kay started to think how terrific it would be if a company could satisfy women's desires for serious careers while also respecting their roles as wives and mothers.

Eventually, Mary Kay's frustration with the situation at Stanley Home Products became unbearable. She knew that she deserved to be promoted to a management position, but being a woman held her back. Her branch manager simply refused to promote her. "I began to see that my whole world was being hemmed in by a man who didn't want me to succeed," she recalled in 1985. "Thirty-five years ago you didn't say anything. You just swallowed it."

World Gift Company

When she and her second husband returned to the Dallas area after a year in St. Louis, Mary Kay decided to try a different direct-sales company. She moved to the World Gift Company and, as she puts it, "within a year my unit was doing a major portion of the company's total business."

Five years later, Mary Kay suffered from a serious medical problem. She began experiencing muscle spasms in her face that caused one whole side of her face to twist into a grimace – not something that would be very appealing to customers! Never one to give in to weakness, she just covered as much of her face as possible with a large pair of sunglasses and went on working. Doctors found that the condition was caused by facial nerves becoming twisted around a blood vessel, and they were able to correct it with an operation.

Although she stayed with World Gift for nine years, Mary Kay encountered the same stubborn prejudices against women that she had experienced at Stanley Home Products. She rose to the position of national training director, with a salary of $25,000 a year. But she knew that she was *really* performing the job of national sales manager, which should have brought a much higher salary. It angered her that, as she says, "a woman's brains were only worth 50 cents on the dollar in a male-run corporation." It also annoyed her to have her ideas and suggestions ignored.

The last straw came when an efficiency expert hired by World Gift warned the executives that Mary Kay was becoming "too powerful." When the executives tried to slow Mary Kay down and hold her back, she resigned in disgust in 1963. That's when she found herself sitting at her kitchen table with a pencil and some paper, thinking about the qualities of her "dream company."

MOVING AHEAD

After her second husband's sudden death, Mary Kay was in a dilemma. In spite of the warnings of her cautious lawyer and accountant, she wanted to go ahead with her plans for Beauty by Mary Kay, but could she succeed on her own? That's when her family came through for her.

For years, Mary Kay's three children had watched her work and win. They knew better than anyone else how much intelligence, energy, and plain old grit she possessed. On the day of her husband's funeral, they showed the same quiet confidence in her abilities that her mother had shown so long ago when she said, "You can do it, Mary Kay."

Her younger son, Richard, was twenty years old and earned a good salary as an insurance salesman. As young as he was, he had a brilliant understanding of money and management. Mary Kay knew that if she was to make her company a success without the help of her husband, she would need Richard's help. But the highest salary she could offer him was only a little more than half of what he was making with the insurance company.

Richard Rogers gave up a promising career in insurance to work for his mother's new company. It was a good decision – he became one of the top executives in the nation. He appears here with Mary Kay at the company's annual awards night in 1988, the 25th anniversary of Mary Kay Cosmetics. (Mary Kay Cosmetics, Inc.)

However, because Richard believed that his mother's potential was unlimited, he accepted the position as Mary Kay's right-hand man. Her older son, Ben, offered to contribute his savings to help his mother get started. Then, a few months later, he too went to work for Mary Kay. And her daughter, Marylyn, also worked for the company until illness forced her to retire.

With the support and encouragement of her children buoying her up, Mary Kay proceeded with her plans. Beauty by Mary Kay would start up on schedule. She had her skin-care formulas and $5,000, the bulk of her own savings, to use as **capital.** Just months after retiring from one successful career, she was in business again – this time for herself.

Capitalization

Mary Kay started her company with a slender stock of capital: a handful of skin-care formulas and $5,000. Even though $5,000 was worth more in 1963 than it is today, it was not much money with which to start a new business. Out of it, Mary Kay had to pay to have her products manufactured, buy containers for them, rent offices and warehouse space, and pay her son's salary.

The costs of all of these things have increased over the years. As Mary Kay remarks, "I think it's important to note that while we started Mary Kay Cosmetics with $5,000 capital, it would take a lot more than that now."

Each year, thousands of **entrepreneurs** like Mary Kay launch their own businesses. Many of them have bright ideas for new or improved products or services to sell to the public. Others are determined to stand on their own two feet and be their own bosses. Yet more than half of all new business ventures fail, most of them during the first year.

Why? According to the government's Small Business Administration, the biggest reason for failure is **undercapitalization,** or starting out without enough capital. Overnight successes are rare. Most businesses need time to catch on. Entrepreneurs who jump into busi-

> ness without enough capital are forced to cut
> corners on their products or services, or to go
> out of business before they have had enough
> time to become successful.

Opening Day

Mary Kay must not be superstitious, because she officially opened Beauty by Mary Kay on a day that is traditionally supposed to bring bad luck: Friday the 13th! That date in September of 1963, however, seems to have brought Mary Kay plenty of good fortune. Each September 13, beauty consultants from all over the country flock to Dallas to celebrate the anniversary of the founding of Mary Kay Cosmetics.

The company operated out of a small office in a business mall and rented storage space in the basement. Mary Kay insisted that Richard dress in a professional manner, so he always wore a jacket and tie in the office. But after a sale was made, he would politely say, "Excuse me for a moment" to the customer in the office and then run down the stairs to the storage area, removing his jacket and tie as he went. Once in the basement, he would gallop to the shelves, assemble the order, put his jacket and tie back on, and run back to the office, trying not to pant for breath as he handed the order to the customer.

After just a year at their first location, Mary Kay and Richard decided to move the business to a larger and more convenient office space. Today, Mary Kay Cosmetics operates out of its own gleaming gold office tower in downtown Dallas.

Mary Kay started off with nine salespeople, or beauty consultants, as they were called. Each of the nine was a friend who joined the business because she trusted Mary Kay's judgment. One of these women, Dalene White, had worked for Mary Kay's husband in the vitamin company and joined Beauty by Mary Kay as a gesture of friendship. That gesture paid a generous dividend to Dalene White. She eventually became a national sales director, and she was one of the first people in the Mary Kay "family" to earn more than one million dollars in commissions.

Chapter 5

Big Business

When Mary Kay and her two sons started out in business, they worked long days and did everything that had to be done. Sometimes they spent sixteen or eighteen hours a day at the office, packing orders, writing letters, typing and mimeographing the newsletter that they sent to all the consultants, and even sweeping the warehouse floor! But the hard work paid off.

After only three and a half months in business, the company had made $34,000 in sales. When operating expenses were subtracted, this left a small but definite profit! Mary Kay must have felt proud – and relieved. Her confidence in her product and in herself was justified.

She felt even more satisfaction at the end of two years of business, when the company had sold an astonishing $800,000 worth of products. Now all she had to do was keep sales climbing upward.

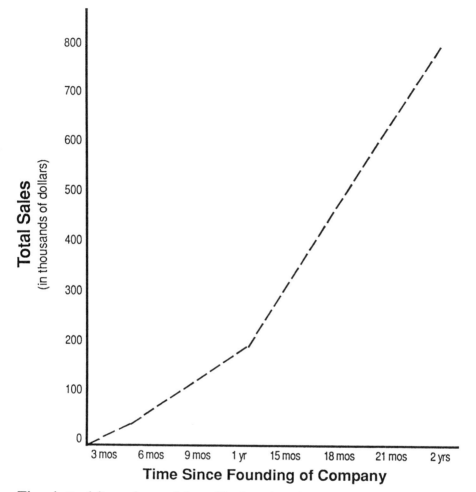

The dotted line shows Mary Kay's sales during her first two years of business. At the end of two years, sales had climbed to an encouraging $800,000.

GROWTH MILESTONES

The growth of Mary Kay's company over the years has been recognized by financial experts as one of the true success stories of American business. A number of milestones mark stages in the history of Mary Kay Cosmetics.

At first, Mary Kay's product line – that is, the assortment of individual products the company offered for sale – was small. It consisted of the five original skin-care lotions and a few "glamour" products, such as lipstick and eyeshadow. Mary Kay bought the glamour products from various manufacturers and paid a local chemical plant to produce the lotions.

In 1968, however, Mary Kay Cosmetics began building its own plant in Dallas for manufacturing its skin-care and beauty products. The manufacturing operation has been expanded several times over the years. Today, the manufacturing building is as large as three football fields and has laboratories, packaging and mailing departments, and warehouse space as well as production facilities. About 450 employees work in the manufacturing plant, which can produce 48,500 jars of cleansing cream every ten hours. The product line today consists of more than 150 items, and almost all of them are made at the company's own plant.

Another important milestone also took place in 1968. That year, Mary Kay's company went public and offered shares of stock for sale. The stock sold so well that Mary Kay became a millionaire. Although the stockholders now owned the company, Mary Kay and Richard themselves owned so many shares of the stock that they continued to control the growth of the company. Mary Kay was its chairman, or top official, and Richard was its president, the next-highest position.

A Third Marriage

Mary Kay had a milestone of her own in 1966, when she married for the third time. Her new husband was Mel Ash, a sales representative whom she met through a friend. Their marriage

Private and Public Companies

Mary Kay Cosmetics started out as a private company, then became a public one, and then a private one again. Private and public ownership each offers different advantages to a company, and each involves different responsibilities.

A private company is just what its name suggests. It can be owned by an individual, a family, or a group of people. Shares of a private company are not available to the general public. And a private company is not required to tell the public how much money it earns or how its money is spent.

A company goes public when it divides its ownership into many portions, or shares, and sells them publicly. These shares are called stock. The value of the stock varies from day to day, depending upon how many people want to buy it and what they are willing to pay for it. Selling stock, or "going public," can be a tremendous advantage to a growing company if it brings a large amount of money into the company, as happened with Mary Kay Cosmetics.

The stock can be bought by either individuals or other companies that want to invest in the company. Those who purchase shares are called shareholders or stockholders. The company's directors and executives are

> responsible to the shareholders for the com-
> pany's performance.
>
> So that people who buy stock will know
> how their investment is being used, each pub-
> licly owned company is required by govern-
> ment regulations to publish reports of its
> earnings and expenses four times a year. These
> are called quarterly reports. Once a year, the
> company must publish an annual report. This
> gives an account of the company's earnings
> and expenses for the whole year, as well as
> highlights of the year and plans for the future.

was a very happy one, and Mel took an enthusiastic interest
in his wife's company. He died in 1980 of lung cancer.

Since Mel Ash's death, Mary Kay has supported cancer
research with grants of money and her services as a fundraiser.
True to her lifelong interest in helping women, she has concentrated on supporting research into the prevention and treatment of breast cancer, which afflicts one out of every ten
women in the United States. In 1990, she served as the hon-
orary chairperson of the Texas Crusade for the American Cancer Society.

The 1970s

Mary Kay Cosmetics flourished during the 1970s. Sales
skyrocketed, new beauty consultants were recruited at a rapid
rate, and the value of each share of stock in the company in-

creased by 670 percent between 1973 and 1983 (this means that if a share had been worth $10 in 1973, it was worth $67 in 1983). The company made money for everyone who had invested in its stock.

The 1970s were also a time of expansion. In 1970, the company opened a regional distribution center, so that not all of the products had to be shipped from Dallas to the beauty consultants around the country. Today, there are distribution centers in California, Georgia, New Jersey, and Illinois in addition to Texas.

The 1970s also brought the company's first overseas business ventures. Under Richard's leadership, Mary Kay Cosmetics opened branches in Australia and elsewhere. Although these international operations were not at first as profitable as had been expected, Richard nevertheless persisted in his plan to open doors for Mary Kay Cosmetics around the world. Today, there are branches in Australia, Canada, Argentina, and West Germany, and plans are being made to open branches in Mexico and other countries.

Honors, Awards, and Books

Mary Kay's achievements as an entrepreneur were recognized by the world of business. In 1976, she was appointed to the Direct Marketing Association's Hall of Fame, and she was also named as one of America's Top 100 Corporate Women by *Business Week* magazine. Over the following years she received many more honors and awards, and Mary Kay Cosmetics was considered one of the most successful companies in the country. In 1984, a book called *The 100 Best Companies to Work for in America* listed Mary Kay Cosmetics.

Back in 1963, when she had begun making her lists of the good and bad things about companies, Mary Kay had planned to write a book. That book was never written, because she used her ideas for her own company instead. But in 1981 she finally did write a book – her life story, or autobiography.

And because she received so many requests to explain how her company had become so successful, Mary Kay published a second book in 1984. It was called *Mary Kay on People Management.* In it she shared her business philosophy and her opinions on how to recruit and motivate people. This book became a best-seller, as corporate executives around the world studied the secrets of Mary Kay's success.

GOING PRIVATE

In the mid-1980s, Mary Kay and Richard decided that they wanted to return the company to private ownership. That is, they wanted to buy up all the shares of stock and make it a family business once again. This was a good time for such a move, because the company had gone into a slight slump and the price of the stock had dropped somewhat. In 1985, all the publicly owned shares were purchased by Richard, and Mary Kay Cosmetics once again became a private company.

That same year, Mary Kay's personal share of the company was estimated to be worth about $26 million. Also in 1985, she built a new home in Dallas, where she frequently entertains the company's top sales directors. It cost four million dollars and has 30 rooms – and it is, not surprisingly, painted pink.

Mary Kay congratulates the woman who has just been crowned "Queen of Personal Sales" at a company awards convention. Remembering how she had worked hard to win sales awards early in her own career, Mary Kay has always rewarded her top salespeople with lavish gifts and plenty of praise. (Shelly Katz/Black Star.)

In 1987, Mary Kay named herself chairman emeritus of Mary Kay Cosmetics. In this position, she is responsible for continuing to uphold the company's philosophy and values and for masterminding its motivational programs for employees and beauty consultants. Richard is chairman of the company.

By 1990, Mary Kay Cosmetics – the company that had started with a mother and a son and a rented room in a mall – had 1,200 employees in its manufacturing plant, office tower, and distribution centers, and about 200,000 independent beauty consultants. The consultants, however, are not employees of the company. Rather, they are self-employed.

Each consultant purchases products from the company at **wholesale** prices and sells them to customers at **retail** prices. The difference between these two prices – usually about double the wholesale price – is the consultant's profit. But although each consultant runs an independent business, all of them are encouraged to attend seminars, conventions, and sales meetings run by the company. And each of them is considered part of the Mary Kay "family" by the company's founder, who claims that she will never lose the personal touch that made her a success in the first place.

Chapter 6

The Lesson of the Bumblebee

Mary Kay Ash has undoubtedly achieved success in material terms. As a young mother, she struggled to support her family, and later she mastered the challenges of direct sales and struggled to make her way in a business that did not encourage women to excel. At a time of life when many people would have retired, she started her own company and amassed a substantial fortune. Yet Mary Kay feels that the financial rewards she has won are just one part of what she has done with her life. Her personal statement of values is "God first, family second, career third."

As a young housewife, Mary Kay taught Sunday School. Religion and the Baptist church have remained important in her life. She has served on many church committees and led many fundraising drives for the church, in addition to her own contributions.

Mary Kay Ash at home in Dallas. She compares the astonishing success of her company to the flight of the bumblebee. Experts say that the bumblebee should not be able to fly – but it goes ahead and flies anyway. (Shelly Katz/Black Star.)

Mary Kay's career in direct sales was the result of her desire to have a job that would let her spend time with her children. She designed Mary Kay Cosmetics so that women with children to take care of can work as much or as little as they want, full-time or part-time. They can schedule their working hours around the time they need to spend with their families.

Because of all the opposition she encountered when trying to build a career, Mary Kay knows that many women are never encouraged to achieve their full potential as employees or independent businesspeople. "We [Mary Kay Cosmetics] let a woman learn and grow to her fullest capacity," Mary Kay says, "to be anything she is smart enough to be." She is grateful that she has had the opportunity to help many other women establish their own careers in direct sales.

Mary Kay Cosmetics is noted for the many prizes and awards that are given to beauty consultants and sales directors who achieve certain goals. One of these awards is a symbol that has a special meaning for Mary Kay Ash. It is a diamond pin in the shape of a bumblebee. In a sense, Mary Kay's entire life and work are summed up by the lesson that the bumblebee represents for her. In her own words:

> Within our organization, the bumblebee has become the ultimate symbol of achievement. We selected it because of what the bumblebee represents for all women. You see, years ago, aerodynamic engineers studied this creature and decided that it simply *should not be able* to fly! Its wings are too weak and its body too heavy for flight. Everything seems to tell the bumblebee, "You'll never get off the ground."

But, Mary Kay points out, the bumblebee just goes ahead and flies anyway.

Glossary

business philosophy   The ideas or principles that guide how a person or company does business.

capital   Money or goods that can be used to produce an income; sometimes also means the total value of someone's money and possessions.

commission   A percentage of a sale.

competitive   A product or service that costs buyers about the same amount as other similar products or services; also, someone who likes to compete.

cosmetology   The sciences and skills involved in inventing, making, and using cosmetics.

delegate   To assign tasks to someone else.

direct sales   A type of selling in which the salesperson contacts the customer directly, without waiting for the customer to go to a store.

efficiency expert   Someone who studies the way a company or an individual works, and then gives advice on how that company or individual could do more work in less time – that is, be more efficient.

entrepreneur   Someone who organizes and runs his or her own business.

executive   A high-level official of a company, usually someone who helps make the company's business decisions.

Great Depression   A period during the 1930s of low economic activity in the United States, with much unemployment.

hard sell   Aggressive, high-pressure sales techniques that sometimes verge on bullying, confusing, or forcing a customer into buying a product.

invest   To spend money (or time, or other resources) in the hope of getting a larger amount back.

marketing   Identifying what particular parts of the population would be interested in a certain product or service, or coming up with ways to interest new kinds of customers in a product or service.

motivate To encourage or inspire someone to accomplish something.

product An item or service that can be offered for sale.

profit In general terms, any sort of benefit. In business terms, the money that comes from selling a product after the costs of buying, making, or selling the product have been subtracted.

recruiting Acquiring workers or employees.

retail The price paid for a product by the end user, or customer, who purchases it for personal use.

soft sell A sales technique that uses suggestion and gentle persuasion.

undercapitalization Insufficient capital to keep a business operating until it has a chance to earn money.

wholesale The price of products purchased from manufacturers that will later be resold to individual customers.

Index